Reverend Harold R. Jarrot Sr.
and Family

Thank you so much
for allowing me to come and s—
with the congregation I pray that
God would bless in abundance your
family and your ministry Sincerely

[signature] II

For 2005

Through the Eyes of a Manchild
B R I D G E S

by

Joe Gofoe II

authorHOUSE®

AuthorHouse™
1663 Liberty Drive, Suite 200
Bloomington, IN 47403
www.authorhouse.com
Phone: 1-800-839-8640

First published by AuthorHouse   9/11/2008

ISBN: 978-1-4343-7783-8 (sc)
ISBN: 978-1-4343-7784-5 (hc)

Printed in the United States of America
Bloomington, Indiana

This book is printed on acid-free paper.

In Loving and Living memory of Derrick,
Eddie, Kendra, Geraldine, Theodore

Table of Contents

Warm Up — 1

Poems never given to people — 25

Third Bridge — 49

Day Dreams 51

God is love — 79

Turning Points of Love 81

Warm Up

Beginning at the top I am a man of God.
My life belongs to him, as well as everything I possess
Although this talent surfaced through an infatuation, there it does not remain
It has been several years since, I have vented, and
been years since I have changed my life
'Through the Eyes of a Manchild' holds much meaning to me
It is about bridges
The bridge between a boy and a man
And the bridge between a man, and God
That is why this book has become a testimony
It is about progression of the mind, and spirit
Looking into past and then present notions of love,
imagination, infatuation, anger, pain
And misconceptions of
My first chapter entails pieces of myself
During conflict
In and out my struggles

Pieces Of The Puzzle

Bound

Strapped and chained
I'm in the prison of my own brain
Self hate and delinquency a prison they do make
I've made many mistakes
Hating every day and depressed every night
I'm the only one keeping myself in the devils' plight
Never completely happy, never satisfied
Last night I had a lot of fun, last night I felt like crying
Can barely express emotion
To nothing I show devotion
Lost by choice in the midst
Wrong choices are the only thing keeping me from heavens bliss
My entire life seems like purgatory
Through fake smiles no one could imagine my sad story
I feel buried by 6ft of dirt, trapped inside
I'm living now, would the world even blink if I died
Time doesn't even show me mercy
Today I'm almost a man, yesterday I was thirteen
Need my heart to be filled, hear loves sweet sound
If I could only remove these chains, by my sins I am bound

Lust

Want it but can't have it
See it but can't stab it
Smell it but I can't proceed
Why on earth do I have such a need?
To control a woman's desired peak
Have her to the point at which she can't speak
It's soaking wet and I haven't even begun yet
I am lustful
Try to hang out in groups but,
No matter what, it ends up being just two
What am I to do?
When it seems I fit the shoe
To be all the good and bad things people think of me
Stressed and close to misery
I am lustful
Enough tension to put footprints on the moon
It's been about three months; it's a place I'll be visiting soon

Stress/**God**

The walls are collapsing

I am God

Drama is something I seem to be attracting

Through fire I
will make you

I pray for this dark cloud to disperse

I am your cornerstone
none can break you

Continuing this path will turn my ride into a hearse

Pleasure in the morning
will surpass the pain

Since the day of my birth I've never felt such pain

That is why my son came

Not even this smoke can dry up all the rain

I know you, and
you haven't lived

I doubt I'll ever be the same

Follow my path and
you will see how it is

Tame is all the hate and passion in my life

To live

Carrying burdens seems to be my people's plight

To love

Hard to give praise for being blessed

For me

When all I feel in this heart of mine is *Stress*

I am

Different side to me

Doubts in my mind
Behind this curtain I can no longer hide
No one can see inside me
If something's wrong what could it possibly be
Everything on the outside seems all right
Laughing and such,
Sun has to be shining bright
A quiet storm
Inside is incomplete, something broken, something torn
Since I was born possessed of urges that shouldn't be known
These thoughts had me trapped felt just like I was owned
Just for a loan, some clarity of thought, I'd pay a high toll
I was told its' just the hearts of man; still none of this puzzle unfolds
Looking from the outside in I was disgusted
So much lust, hate, and greed how can I be trusted
Easier to push it down deep
And just hope through the cracks it doesn't seep
Every time I close my eyes these images of a lustful past reside
Sometimes it doesn't help to ask why
To pray I close my eyes
Even then to my mind these images fly
It makes me concentrate harder, to speak to the Father
Petrifying my mind making it impenetrable of thoughts that could bother
No ones fault but mine
Messing with girls instead of recess and tag on my mind
I don't have forever to change
Hope with time, my heart won't stay the same

Section of thought

Walking along this path I have chosen
My minds open
Planting my feet in steps not my own
I never have been
And never will be alone
In my struggles
In my nighttime's
In my thought rhymes
In my sacrifice, which is my life
Every second of every minute of every hour
I dedicate to Christ
In my sacrifice
I died to the world
No more ... drinking and gambling
No more ... hustle and scheming
No more ... squares and blunts
No more fornication
Going on for about a year
5 months ... 3 weeks ... 5 days ... 14 hours ... 35 minutes, and 13... 14 seconds
But who's counting
I'm counting
But in truth it's not the days or hours
Its pleasing God
Who daily gives me a shower in blessings
Never leaves me guessing
But with a hundred and fifty % of content in my heart
From his side I will never depart
On his path
And his word I will last
That's why I don't have to be first I can be last
I don't need mine now,
For my every thirst, my every desire
Will be matched and exceeded
Lighting my fire
Dulling my senses
Without getting bent, without getting lit
Totally conscious, that's just a piece of my life and that's how I'm living it

Dear Lord

Dear Lord break these chains
Dear Lord break these bricks I don't want a
Tower of sorrow I just need a place to sit
And build upon these foundations you've laid
I got to think up on ways on how to get paid
Without getting sprayed
I got to come up with ways to increase my revenue
Without leaving my soul stained by sins residue
I know I can't control the wind
That's why I keep my hopes in check
Having no fear of death, because only the
Wind can bend trees, and we your people are printed on
Forever, covered by dust paper
Draped in mortal hours, I have no tears left
There are wicked tongues at my back
And clever quizzes in my ear
I am being seduced by sorrow
From flesh to marrow
My senses tell me the enemy is near
Just to keep from losing faith
I search and ingest your living word
Filling my soul with your power made perfect in my weakness
But dear Lord a still feel connected
And it's hard to ignore
I feel a knocking inside
I can't quite reach the door
I hear echoes of soothe - sayers
And mothers prayers
Shots in the sky
Flaming arrows cross my pathway, more often than not
Not even in my daymares does it stop
In the midst of this message I had a vision
Though explicit and vivid
I was on top of earth
And as far as I could see to the right
As far as I could see to the left
I saw millions of people wearing t -shirts that read death
In my attempts to step forward and free them from their bond
I saw that I myself was hand in hand arm in arm
With no strength
So I spoke into being the freedom that was mine
I lifted my voice to the heavens

In Jesus name I will break these chains
In Jesus name I will break these bricks
I will no longer be a ripple in the sea of this world
Never again will I sit among the tents of wickedness
Silent, now free from restraint I will
Charge to the hills and in a loud voice proclaim
Devil let my people go
You are defeated
Let my people go
No I'm not conceited
This strength is not my own it lies within Christ
The resurrected
My source of life
Dear Lord, help me to break these chains.

Running

As I look around this place
Without harmony
I see for me there is no space
No where to lay my weary body
I can't see
I can't even imagine
Someone caring where I may be
So I am running
Racing against time for it doesn't belong to me
Running past the hills and where the horizons be
Chased by clouds following the trail that I run
I am running for a purpose, hardly for fun
I am racing against ignorance
Nipping at the heels of knowledge
Racing against irresponsibility
While grabbing the back of manhood's' shirt
As if that wasn't enough
While the past knowledge of woman is rubbing my face in the dirt
Grit other men have done in the past
I am running with the wrath of women with a flame to my... as I stagger,
Racing time, time ant time again to define
My life while in existence, I must live it according to the divine
But I am running out of time
The grains are receding every minute
Regardless of weather or not I finish
I'm in it, heels over head
Being the benefactor of bad knees to keep running I dirty my dreads
Now I am running to find a place
Asking God, pleading with Him to hear my case
Racing against evil because it's gunning
Deep inside I know that is the real reason that... I am running

Going Against the Wind

I'm holding on tight, not about to be taken without a fight. Holding on tight to truth, for lies always catch up to their maker. While lust herself gets dressed up nice and wants me to date her. Can I get a minute to breathe? That woman is hawking me by day, and by night in my dreams she has been stalking me. It was bad before, but now she follows me wherever I go. If that wasn't enough, you should feel this other wind that's blowing in town. I'm surrounded in an environment under the rule of Mr. Hypocrite. Who never misses a beat, if I were able I would knock him back conscious. My cause is for good reason for that old mans' purpose is fast asleep. Sleep on humanity; sleep on reality, wondering blindly each and every day throughout society. They both grow in strength twisting and bending, through their strongest winds it's me they've been sending. Attempting to make me part of their hole, not realizing that I chose to try and walk the paths of old, the lessons that through the Bible were told. Trying, I swear just to live my life right, trying not to be a puppet of the devil, going against the light. That light is my only guide to that truth. So onto that I cling. Knowing that only happiness that light can bring. But that must offend those winds because they are blowing like crazy. So I just keep fighting, and going against the wind.

Above
With all the evils that surround us on earth
Why does it seem to be only the rich man's turf
Living my life humble doesn't require me to live poor
But why is righteousness while rich such a struggle for
Feeling guilty for taking advantage of pleasures of the flesh
A war in itself to remember that our lives on Earth are only a test
When I pray I ask to be lifted above...
Above the evil spirits dwelling on Earth
No longer witness to the destruction of childbirth
Above the hate
The further I go the more color lines disintegrate
Above adultery
Where me and my wife can be her and me only
Above the planned destruction of people and cultures on Earth
Who where forced to work despite snow and till the dirt
Above,
      Earth,
          Space,
              And Time,
No material things, near Him nothing I own would be worth a dime
Nothing but my love for the eternal, the everlasting
With His love...Above

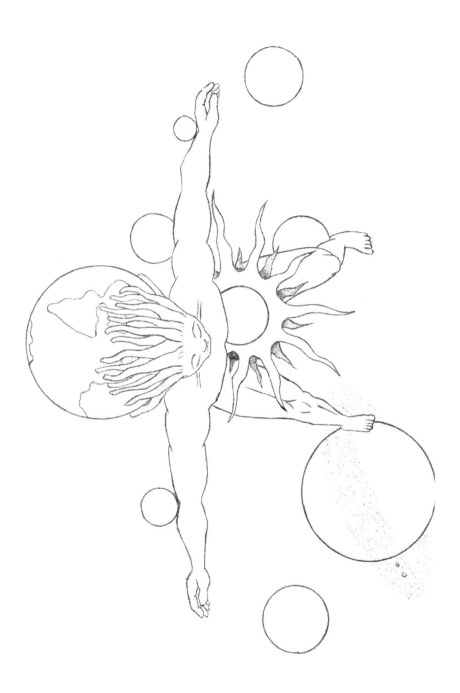

Provision
Brittle is the base of operation of Want
Weary from the same old loop
It's what you might call an imaginations stunt
Blindly
Leaping off of the hand I was dealt
Was the saturation of anticipation
Being submerged in what I once before,
Or simply never had felt
Witness to what was needed
Had it
But wants, easily exceeded
So to get it, I had to get it
And if I had to live it, so be it
I had to live it
Of course to my visuals it was all splendid
Come to find out
Before it began it was all finished
Thereafter
Living was as a condition
The devils confusion
Looking good, but
Only as long as I was sinning
No matter how I cut it, I just wasn't living
My base crumbled
As all else followed
A shell of a man
Victim to these hands
Made to begin again in green pastures
Now serving the Master of all creation
Even as
Unworthy
Tainted
Blind
To be
Cleansed
Free from sin
Given new eyes
No longer composed of wants
Unbound from the chains that accompany skin

The game is fixed, I said yes,
And victory comes at the end
Pride is in the fire
Content is sitting on top of the mantle
Just as the flowers of the field
I have provision

My hour
By choice I am alone, or is it by misfortune
Because any self -proclaimed love I have inside is constantly erased
Taken to court to battle with this wolf inside of me
It's gotten to the point where I'm fed up, and simply tired of being me
Always 2 days walk away from being content
Yet I'm always doing the walking, Can't someone just meet me half?
Love is built up with no release, only the 4 winds tame the angered beast
It yearns to be released, just for a day, cleanse my heart relieve my mind
It's imperative in order to keep the old me at bay
Drop a couple of old habits, and let myself be heard
My usual routine is for the birds, its time to take authority
Re-up and consider what the outcomes my be
Hunt my prey and devour, Fill my spirit with swords, show my power
Learn to love God first, be patient, because for clarity this is my hour

Short strand

If I had to be a string of grass, I'd probably be one of the short ones,
Straight low key, undercover you might say
You would never catch that sun beating down on me all day
Nikes, timberlands, Adidas, none of them would trample me
They wouldn't have to try to cut me down, make me fit their mold
If I have to be seen, I want this whole world to see me
Not the image of any potential, just another number lost in the sea
No animals could reach, and commence to devour my very being
Leaving my roots as my only trace,
I couldn't just be unoccupied space
I need to have a face, unique and undeniable characteristics
Not just a landfill, or part of a child's mud mix
I want sometimes at least to have the upper hand
So I'll do what I have to do, and be the short strand

My All

I hear by declare that I will give my all
On my word I say it
The only thing that's mine I can call
Fall I might but stand down never.
Not the most intelligent,
But in my heart and faith I am clever
To my fellow man I give my all
For all my loved ones & ancestors I stand tall
I promise to love and not hate,
Except the hand I've been dealt embrace my fate
Try to create, a pathway for other people,
For Jesus did the same for me.
And when I find my wife there will never be a reason
To separate me from thee
Nothing on this earth will receive more love than the Father
I'll give my all cause to love a wretch like me he did bother

Stones and sticks
All men are dogs
They all break and don't fix
Stones and sticks
You need to lose a little weight
You're getting fat in the face
You sure are polite
You're a credit to your race
Stones and sticks
You procrastinate
Confused adolescent
Appearance is mature
In my heart I know it's fake
Stones and sticks
You're not a hero
You won't last
Same old Joe
I know the secrets of your past
Stones and sticks
Are you really afraid of nothing, short of the wrath of God?
Or are you scared of women too
Because you didn't even feel up that young brawd
Stones and sticks

No drink no smoke
The Bible
This is no joke

No matter how well you do
There will always be problems that you alone can't fix
Words are either good or evil
Stones and sticks are just another one of the devils' tricks!

Born unto the sun
I am born unto the sun
With strength and endurance
My body is warm
Vision focused
My will to shine is my only insurance
This umbilical cord feeds me daily
With light and knowledge
Witness this miracle and pay homage
For I am born unto the sun
But stars burn out
And fall from the sky
But like the phoenix and Maya Angelo "I rise"
From the ashes I was reborn
Formed from something lifeless
As a child weak and sightless
Confused
Without purpose
Until by God I was used
First breath was as fire
First step as an earthquake
Of rhythms I was the baseline
I'm not a lion, but at my first words rivers did shake
Making of me
A vessel, in all entirety
My reflection is not what I once wished to be
Realizing it was tainted
Now knowing, I'm in the image,
And serving he that is in and all around me
Defending me
Learning me
Always concerned for me
I am a conqueror
Mentoring children
God's the sponsor
Now I'm a man
Not because of my age
But because nothing on earth can turn my page
I'm rooted in stone
Carved out of wood

I walk on commandments
My mental state is as it should be
Defying statistics
And straying from the majority
What I'm becoming will be complete in the end
My pathway is narrow
But I know that it's right
It will come accompanied by physical death and my soul's eternal life

Just Joe
Who am I just Joe
And what I'm for is justice
And where I'm from it's just us
Brothers and sisters of Christos I am
I am nothing born from dust plus
Breath blown straight from the lungs of God
So with each and every single breath I take
His existence, His presence, and my purpose are confirmed
When I'm gone I don't want a tombstone
Just plant a seed
Because while I'm here, that's what I'll be doing planting seeds
Yielding crops full of shepherds and soldiers and martyrs
No I don't want to suggest that I'm powerful
But tomorrows not promised
So rather than being sorrowful over my fleshly limitations
I try to show myself a workman approved
Leaving my Father and your Father with a sense of satisfaction
It's time for wake up like Foldgers not time for make up
Face the facts God is real
The ways of this world is an attack our enemy reveals himself in abundance
You must use and access both hemispheres seeking foundation
Fear not your limitations
Restrain from all temptations
The Father is waiting
Who am I even to suggest
I am nothing
I was nothing until the Spirit entered my cup
What was once empty is now constantly overflowing
If it seems like I'm different it's not the dog in me sweetheart
There is no dog in me
It's the God in me
O say can't you see, the clock is winding down
The king awaits His appointed time to scorch the surface of the earths ground
Our children are listening to our speech
Their eyes know what our walk is really like
And that's why they watch TV in search of a real world a real life
With some consistency
Rather than a half in half out contradictory walk
That don't line up with the scriptures that Jesus has taught
Who am I it don't even matter
I'm just Joe seeking justice from the only one who's ever been just
And where I'm from I'll never go back
Look to the walk of Jesus
It's not the religion; it's his passion that we lack

Poems never given to people

Poems never given to people
Words never spoken to people
Hurts never known to people
Silence was once a barrier for my feelings' protection
I never really liked the attention that came along with depressing matters
I used to see it as; Life is life, so swallow it
Not knowing that God would take away the hurt
Replacing it with peace
Now knowing that prayer is the key
I do not fear expressing what is heavy on my heart
I have no fear of rejection
And silence no longer knows my name
This chapter is a roller coaster of emotion
Those that purge the deep
And those that scratch the surface of the shallow end

Dedicated to…
In remembrance of…
Just for you's…

See Through

I can see you,
But to you I'm see through
In your eyes I don't exist
Without me you believe life will be bliss
What kind of thoughts are these
Hoping you can take me out with the disease of addiction
When I'm not paying attention
What kinds of stunts do you pull?
When you single me out in school,
Trying to take me out with your many tools
Brain washed fools that were once brothers to me
And make it so they try to drug me up
It's bad enough they don't have sense of themselves
But, you take their hopes, and dreams, and place them on the shelf
Your trophy and your reward
Then they try to take me to where those devils be
I just don't understand,
There is only one race and that's the race of man
How can I explain all these things to you
When I can see you, but to you I'm see through

A brief tribute

I wouldn't dare attempt to write a poem about women
For there are no words to compare
Nor would any action
Because anything attempting to define, would certainly be lacking
Centuries of discovery
To most problems a woman has been the solution
Losing a woman is like losing an entire limb
Science can help a little, but a man will never quite be the same again
Instead, I will offer a word
Or a phrase behind each letter in the word woman
To pay respect, because without them there would be no continuance of man
W- Stands for willful, standing for something, not just falling for anything
O- Is for original, spawning from no molds, all individuals
M- Is for maternity, carrying, conceiving, and raising any way they can
A- Stands for adaptation, to the world, and the ever-changing ways of man
N- Has and always will stand for nurture
Without which the earth wouldn't rotate
For without being witness to that love, the love of a woman
The earth would be truly be in a sad state

Power of praise
Open your eyes and see children of Abraham
God inhabits the praises
Of those who seek the Son of man
Even though we've been shaped in iniquity
And this world is fallen
Praise with your whole heart and listen because the Father calling
The well that we drink from, it quenches our thirst
Because before we drink we speak praises to His name
For today as surely as the sun rises
A man may be broken
And tomorrow God can mold him into
Something more than dust
Something more than just a toiler of the fields
A conqueror that is ready for battle and never yields
It is a transformation
Induced by the proclamation
Jesus is the Christ died for our sin
Buried and resurrected
With all authority
Calls us from the majority
To be His bride
It is this realization
That brings us to the place we're supposed to be
In our quiet place
Standing, on our face, or down on our knees
Arms in full surrender
And our mouths filled with praise
Where the Spirit of the living God dwells
Our moment of truth
Our place of deliverance
The destruction of strongholds
The healing of sickness
Where lame shall walk
The blind shall be given clarity
These things take place when
God is given the glory with all sincerity
Won't you just open your eyes and see children of Abraham
God inhabits the praises
Of those who seek the Son of man
Even though we've been shaped in iniquity
And this world is fallen
Praise with your whole heart and listen because the father is calling

Candle Light

Before you read this I must make a request,
I don't want you to read this with worries on your chest
When your day is all done, and of peace your heart has some
Jump in the tub, on your bed place fresh linen,
Let loose your mind, don't fight just listen
Leave some space on the dresser
Or table closest to your bed
And right before you lay down your head,
Light a candle, and slightly crack the window
Break out this poem I wrote below,
Especially for your intellectual stimulation
And read it to quench the temptation,
To let the mind wonder where it will
So lay your body to rest and let your imagination take control

Candle Light
As the flame flickers
Slightly disturbed by a cool breeze
Goose bumps begin to flow from your neck,
And proceeds down to your knees
Darkness barely exists
Dancing between the light of the candle
And that of the moon
Yet that radiant candle catches your eye
The flame gentle, not too bright
It dances against the wall
Caresses the contours of your skin
The state of mind your in is one of satisfaction
When rolling over is your only action
Relaxing every inch of you
While your wishing the love of your life to be there
One hand inching across your waist
The other stroking your hair
Your focuses are each other
But along with one another
The silent candle
Producing just enough light, for two
Lighting your way to love
It can lead your imagination
To places your future is waiting
It has enriched my life, I hope it lights yours too
What wonders candlelight will do

People

We on the rise
No limits have control of us
Advancing past the skies
We headed for the stars
Not forgetting our past scars
But the future looks too bright to dwell on the past
Tomorrow's ours at last
We aren't a race, just a people
There is only the race of man
But they just don't understand because to them we see through
So my people don't get too comfortable
Don't be too content
Because while the movements on
We got to get all we can get
Not just sit back and get bent
And wonder where our lives have went
A misguided youth and forgotten future, due to a forgotten past
We have to reinforce knowledge through our seeds
And make sure that an entire village is not just what our children needs
But has in their lives
Let's give our praises to the skies
Come on my people we on the rise

Pray Mother
Tears form into rivers
In the middle of the night
Voice so quiet
So still
It can't be heard among the waters
Then the words move
Stretching across floorboards
Climbing chairs
Scaling shadows
And jumping though windows
Up higher
Higher, and even higher
Until those words streamline the heavens
Up past the atmosphere
Where the stars appear as crystal
And vibrant full of light
Around moons and the pathways of comets
All the way to eternity
That forever
That beginning
Without end
Where words transform
Into heavenly scents
From the dusty floor boards
Sweat and tears
Intercession
Down on her knees a mother prays
Not for herself
But for those she loves
Pray Mother

ER

My heart throbbed
As I felt for the door knob
Didn't know what to expect
From this, I wish him, I could protect
Grandpa looked so weak
Hardly able to get to his feet
Made me unable to explain what I felt, whole room felt tight
As I sat on his side offered silent prayers' into the light
Unable to sit at first
Uncomfortable, frustrated and waiting to burst
His countenance is one of pain
The sight of that made my eyes want to drain
My mind surprisingly not filled with grief
For my heart knew he would surely rise to his feet
What's with all these tubes
Machines and such, images I wish I could elude
Hard to be witness to the hurt, want to do something, feel shame
Praying he would be the same
Unchanged by a stressful experience
Being kept drugged up cause of pain, halfway delirious
Emergency room
At first the very sound made me nervous
Wasn't his time, still in need of his service
This scare I can hide
Way down deep on the inside
That I might have lost someone I love
Come to realize there is nothing to fear, up above
He is now home after weeks' recovery
Want to know him better, make new discoveries
Do everything he wants me to even when pride won't let him admit it
Incredible all the things he's done in his life, he did live it
Now I know the hospital isn't a place to lose hope
But a place for families to be as strong as knots in a rope
Emergency room
Place containing hope and prayers
Yet, a place I pray he won't visit again soon

E

Sometimes beginning is hard from an ending

Losing someone who was so close

A lot of time running the streets we were spending

Long conversations contemplating the earth's many secrets,

But never were there talks of it all ending

No longer feeling whole,

Because to grow old with our children eventually was our goal

It seems E's future was stole

This whole situation is out of control

Cause the pages of life were turning fine

Till I was told my brother close to my heart had just flat lined

How can I eat, and I don't know nobody named sleep

That's supposed to keep my body rested, but I can't help it I'm just restless

Sometimes I just get aggressive and want to hurt something'

I wish the Lord would come down for the purpose of this fallen loved one

But it must not be in his plan for this young man to become a man

I'll just try to carry on

With no attempts to understand, for I am just a young man

I look to God and know everything's all right

Cause since before the time of his birth

Heavens glory was in his sight

Soldiers' song

You can dance to the smoke and lights
But this world don't know it's left from its right
So we sing our soldiers song during the midst of battle
And even before we go to sleep at night
Why? To ignite the torch, what torch?
The one we carry for Yahweh of course
We separate ourselves from the temptations of this flesh
And submit the best as a sacrifice
We say a prayer similar to this
Our father who art in heaven hollowed be thy name
Thine kingdom come thy Will be done on earth as it is in heaven
Give us this day our daily bread
And every word that comes from your mouth
So that I will never hunger again
I am broken before your sight
Give me wings to take flight
Take this vessel consecrate it and mold it into a bowl
So that there can be less of me and more of you
Take this heart and break it
Keep only the portions that see you as sacred
I seek your forgiveness
I will stand, as a soldier should
With my worship having no end
Help your chosen to stand their ground until you come again
Amen
We are composed of parts that hunger and thirst for God eternally
But until we can stand under the wings of His majesty
He gives us water from rock
And bread from heaven
Our rations are always sufficient
Much like His grace
Heaven is sweeter than sweet
Give Him glory and you can have a taste of paradise promised
Within the ranks of He that is before, before
We are an army of one
One Faith, one love, one judge
Though we will never fully attain it
We seek after perfection
Each time we fall there is a lesson
We load it into our Berettas and bust shots at the enemy
Are you hearing me?
When Jesus Christ was tempted He quoted scriptures
After 40 days with no food
The Word alone had enough power to make the devil leave the picture

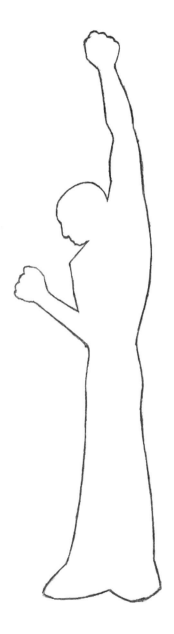

Are you hearing me?
You can try but you won't succeed in halfway fighting a war
We stay prepared
In the armor of God
The Holy Bible is our sword
Our weapon from the divine
Righteousness is on our chest
Salvation covers our mind
We got heavenly gospel issued boots
A shield of faith
Truth itself is wrapped around our waist
Soldiers are never born
They are made
Through time and pressure
We wanted freedom from the monotonous,
We received from above a message that's obvious to us
With all certainty God is just as real as and more important than oxygen
Not just saying it, but believing it
There is no man we fear
You can harm the body but never the soul
Soldiers are never on their own
We salute and wait while the Holy Spirit passes in
It's never tragic when you're in the Will of God
We were cursed, and then he became a curse
Now our faith can be like Moses' rod
As long as we hold it high for all to see
And we'll continue to have the victory
If you're a true soldier let me see you put your fist in the sky
And if your not may God ignite the fire inside
Hear what I say and see with new sight
Life is hard, but not knowing God is the worst of tragedies in life
Calling all soldiers

Melissa

Where to begin
How does one find the words to describe
A lady who Webster himself couldn't define
Athletic as well as poetic in motion
To her faith she shows her devotion
Has the very scent of pleasure
That is only half of the truth
The cause would be the truth
The effect socks blown off, and minds through the roof
Where is my proof
Where to begin
It should be obvious
Because if she was a concert
I would be but a shy lobbyist
I don't want to invade her personal space
But I can't help it
Satisfaction would be found inside her magical stare
Then I would rest my case
For it would be a simple thing
For her to erase the invisible space divider
I have no needs, but for that which is inside her
I suppose I'll end with even more of her truth
Here it goes, a few more lovely characteristics
To see the physical is simple
Addictive smile, coming complete with a set of dimples
Eyes containing the innocence of a child
Brown with secrets,
Enough to drive a brother wild
I would go further, but to protect her honor I'll have to defer
But I will say this to show what state I'm in
With her is my completion
Yet, I don't know where to begin

Black Beauty
You're my black beauty, a diamond without no jewelry
When I get sick your love is what cures me
Eyes so dark and deep it's like the bottom of the sea,
When they glitter & shine that's where those pearls be
Every place that we meet was created for you and me
Don't care about others opinions, what everyone thinks
You touch my hand I pull you close; drama disappears within an eye blink
Lips tastier than chocolate, any problems your love will solve it
Inside a packed room, within your brilliance I become consumed
Can't help but watch, immobilized by your entirety
You have the most beautiful shape
Simply a Kodak size
I'd have to be deprived of all sense not to recognize
Your body is enticing,
But your mind is what has me
Just 'jonesin' off conversation alone
Easy to believe that the very stones envy your strength,
All while your patience can't be measured by street length
Yet, you know when to let go
Your faith and knowledge of this earth is what makes it grow
Africa is the very base of your trees' foundation
You birthed the existence of population, every nation
Is it any wonder why you never leave my mind
You belong by my side never to be left behind
Ability to carry life inside you, respect is always due
Allow me to provide you with any service I can render
You will be what makes my life complete, living in complete splendor
My every desire is within you and you wanting me the same
I'll search the entire earth until I know your name
You are my flower; nothing else could convince me
While I'm searching you will forever and always remain my black beauty

Admirer
Touch my hand
And I shall not stir
Twine your fingers through my hair
And we might have to take it there
Where you ask?
If you have to ask than I shall not tell
Better for the pool of your imagination to dwell upon it
Lap after lap, mile after mile
Sensualology
Millions of possibilities, from a single word
Anything to create that beautiful, and adored smile
Adored you ask?
If you have to ask than I shall not tell
For I speak straight from the heart
And I am that thought
Swimming deep at the base of your well
Spellbound and silenced for an endless moment
Density of memory cells, wondering where the time went
The keeper of that time will be me
Who you ask?
If you ask I might just tell
Just know that my love will sprout wings and take you higher
Truly yours signed,

Your Admirer

Granddad
What I become
I remember he was
What I will learn
I remember he knew
The strength he had
I will soon come to know
The pain I can
But his memory I will never let go

Victory

Forget not, retreat press on through
Plant your roots in Calvary
So you can bring forth fruit
As branches of the true vine
Be among men and not be defined
By his ways, his lust, thirst not for his wine
Envy not his fortune
For his fortress is a fortified prison
That divorces him from the ways of the Father
Rejecting His grace
Face it
Without God man will never make it
If you don't have to believe me
Gleam from the words found in psalms 73
And you will clearly see the reasons why this fight is unique
Because the end is guaranteed

Come, come children
Gather around, forget yourselves and lay your burdens down
Come, come children
Bind your flesh to the altar
Begin to see with a vision that is not your own
Defeat is a whisper; Victory is a war cry from heavens own
This life has an end, Christ is the only way to truly get on
Shoulder to shoulder we will walk
With accountability we speak
Never afraid of the terror that stalks, or roaring lions,
We follow the cornerstone road, and to life scriptures what we're applying
We die daily just to live again
Our victory is assured
And all are welcome to join in

When a poet dies
There is a silence
Things are still
No inspiration until
We look unto the hills
From which commeth our help
And then
Silence falls
Becoming a victim
For written words sprout like maple seeds
And glide through the pages
Of our minds
Glazing them with the sweetness of the
Morning's tears

When a poet dies
A gift that was given
Returns to sender
After fulfilling one's purpose
Beneath the surface would have been found
The fingerprints of God
A blessing was she
And from rib to earth
Was a full and fruitful measure
A written legacy through poetry
The vision God had
Came through the children that she birthed, you see
Life's worth goes beyond worldly measure
It is a pause between eternities
A comma
What perished
Was simply the vessel we could see
The essence, the spirit lives on

When this poet died
Heads were held low
Many tears where shed
Testimony to the difference
And many impressions she made
Time has passed
And everything has seemingly changed
Remember this, she will find life
For Christ already defeated death
Let's not dwell upon her departure
Rather, embrace the fact that she came
Now free from mortal hours
She has moved towards forever
No more bathing in sunlight
But waiting to be called up
To one day be
Christened by the countenance
Of He that is forever
When this poet died she didn't die
We will never forget her
Friend, Wife, and Mother

Third Bridge

Being a book about bridges this chapter is the third bridge
My imagination and reality collaborate
My standing up for youth

When older generations refer to teenagers as "crazy"
I find it hard to disagree, but for different reasons
Transitions are never easy
Going from all is well with the world
Gradually
Or after sometimes being thrust into reality
Should not be taken lightly or seen as something natural
Sometimes traumatizing
Issues come with the territory of age
You see these are things that can build up for years
Fear, hatred, jealousy
Finding out the real reason to be careful of strangers
Why certain family members have to be kept from the kids
Why homes are broken
Abortion
Wars
Stress
Things that if not in a relationship with God
Would cause a foundation to crumble
As these things build they leave a residue on the mind
I cleaned mine off
And put it on paper

Day Dreams

Picture

She walked into his life
And made it anew
She wasn't aware of the damage she was going to do
Became salt to his ice
Turning out the light that was blue
Her song was the truth
Rhymed with his entire life
Making it worth while
Becoming his wife
Under the church light fixture
The couple had taken their wedding picture
It came to be that she was all he needed
Her smile was very addictive
Her legs went on for days
Sorry about that one
She was too beautiful not to get descriptive
She became ill one day and from there it all went down hill
He told the doctors he would pay any bill,
Just make it okay
No medicine on earth could make her live long enough,
To say what he had to say, that he loved her every day
That no one could or would ever take her place
It would remain his and her space
Till this day he swears that woman became his scripture
And with him he always keeps their picture

Bundle of Joy
They tasted of joy that was meant for men and women
It wasn't about the thrust of lust
It was about holding hands and the pleasure of silk when they touched
Performing many protected, coed activities
Late in the day chasing bright horizons
Taking cupids arrows like thieves.
Just as affectionate as the feeling of being born free
Love has given two on this earth a future
Being destined to be a little bit of history
Yet, with a sigh of fear
As such pleasure can't be right
True, and hurtful
They were wrong but made things right
For in the growing of their love
Faith in God was the seed
The need to continue was not a want but a necessity
As if the scene couldn't be more beautiful.
It came to pass that their cup of joy came, and came in full
Nothing could be better growing a seed off loving
They were made complete by God, and having a new bun in the oven

Purple

Purple tied down to tracks
Minus blue equals the color she left behind
If only she had thought of reasons just to be
Then rather than in vain she would be justified

She was not wine from grape
More like orange from concentrate
Produced by unknown field handlers
Hailing from up the block regions
Her home after womb was a glass box
Under developed and 'feening'
For something she never had
Not on purpose anyway
Found hidden in a garbage bin
Abandoned
With no age

Her life was like
Purple tied down to tracks
Minus blue equals the color she left behind
If only she had thought of reasons just to be
Then rather than in vain she would be justified

Somewhere between the mean streets and orphanage
And her foster fathers dope game
The sell of her virtue for his gain
She became a teenage woman
Developed
Now old men is what she's pulling
Curbs, and yellow dashes
Streetlights, and car seats
Passion, spit, and cash
Calling her name
Barely of age
A vet in the game
Her walk don't tell her age
Blade hidden inside her braids
Mama wasn't around to say there'd be better days
So it became cuts for luck

Roulette that's Russian
Shots before noon
Tears at night
She even goes by that garbage bin
That she was abandoned in
And wonders
Why couldn't it all end then
If you're silent
You can hear the wind carrying her cries
And it sounds like

Something like
Purple tied down to tracks
Minus blue equals the colors she left behind
If only she thought of reasons just to be
Then rather than in vain she might be justified

About 30 years in age
And it seems like every time she closes her eyes
Five years passes by
Several pimps done came and went
Still she can't leave seem to leave
So she continued to press her ebony flesh
In keeping with her past
And intertwining her soul with whomever had the cash
Until what was last on her mind became first
She found out that she would give birth
To a child, produced by unknown field handlers
Hailing from up the block regions
What she swore would never happen, happened
She relived her mother's sequence

Her life was like purple tied down to tracks
Minus blue equals the color she left behind
If only she had thought of reasons just to be
Then rather than in vain she might be justified

Holiday Season
I'm giving thanks while standing in the hardships of life
Not needing to see the outcome.
God's will is what I recognize as right
Birthing sight into the equation
I see that I am not alone
And the book that has my destiny
Cleo couldn't read to me over the phone for $9.99 a minute
I'm grateful to God
He makes me stronger than Popeye on two cans of spinach
That's why I'm giving thanks during these holidays
I don't give my thanks to almost pioneers
Who almost discovered this land
If it wasn't for the fact that people were already here
I say Glory to God for being that light
For the hardships in life
Because they teach us humility
And how to fight against temptations
That play tug of war with your mind, covering your eyes
And providing you with a Seeing Eye dog that happens to also be blind
These are the times you can feel it
You're being tested, this isn't the time for pride to become erected
Learn your lessons
Receive your blessings
We all fall down, but that's no reason to stay down
Endurance will one day award you a crown, and a pair of wings
To soar above and beyond all these worldly ways and spirits
God speaks to us daily step forward and you'll hear it
I thank God for a lyric called joy in my mind
And a song called peace in my soul
Pleasing Christ shouldn't be your annual but your daily goal
Patience and wisdom will guarantee you see how things unfold
To your benefit
This is your life follow Christ and start living it
Let's put Columbus and Santa to the side
And give our creator thanks during all times

Tip top

Flowing like water sweat beads
Spreading like goose bumps
Thoughts are as fire, tongue as two swords
And from the tip to the top
He combs over every inch of her body
He couldn't find the courage to stop
Beginning with clear and dark shots
Followed by hollowed cigars
Then to rubbing navels
Tipsy turvy went the tables
Now wearers of labels STD
Jotted down in the obituaries
Not able to fix
Once potential Kings and Queens
Known to the masses today as statistics
Tip top
Cheek full of dope
Gun at waist
Listed on that shotty
Was so many bodies, that even for the combined efforts of the NYPD, LAPD,
GRPD, to keep trace
Not hardly starving, just a little hungry for that paper chase
Then from the top he fell to the tip of law enforcement's boot
Streets was hot, he got knocked but he bonded then went straight back out to the
block
Rather than corners, 'cuz' pumps straight off the bus stop
In his mind he was providing a service
And in doing so made his pockets thick
But from being patient some snakes can get sick
Once he was comfortable and no longer feeling nervous
His last thought was cold steel subject to the next mans service
Tip top
And from the tip to the top we all fall short
Being victims of the tick and the toque
It's a set up
Putting women men and riches on top
Consider your destination
And which way you'll be escorted
I'd rather live in pain, then reap the wages of sin
Pain lets me know God's just working on me again
And the wages of sin, that's just death
Death to the physical, Death eternal,
Instead of hoods, and sets, Jesus the Christ is what we should rep
Holy Spirit dipped
Rather than taste death
Nectar from the tree of life is what we should sip
Tip Top

Jetae
I stare when she's not looking
Turn away when I'm found out
Should I put her on notice?
That I notice her
And want to see what she's all about
Dark skinned tone
Slim but got enough to give off thigh muscle tone
Sat next to her in geometry
And the end of the equation
Her + Me = where I want to be
How can I keep my composure?
I sit near but I want to be closer
And what is killing me is that
It's hot outside and of her skin there is exposure
If I could only just run my fingers down her spine
Pour two glasses of wine, and dine her all evening
And love her all night,
Can she sense my plight?
This isn't love I barely know her
How in the world can I show her without offense
Because when I try to speak she puts up an ice fence
I suppose she has a man that I understand
But she's even shy to speak, only short responses I can land
Give me a few more days and I'll let the whole thing go
Because I pay more attention to her than class
And my grades are starting to show

No Sunrise
Colors golden, darkened blues chased away
Wetness glistens,
From the night is born a new day
Prayers are answered, blessings received
Children are being born,
A man breathes his last breath
The earth is no longer cold
Moon's shadow is destroyed, a new day unfolds
As constant as birth
As true as the earth's revolution
Without it everybody's minds they would be losing
But when the world's time is over,
It will take everyone by surprise, for what will the blind do
When the skies turn gray, and there is no sunrise

Compete

We all compete
Some ways obvious
And some of them discrete
Be it for that all mighty dollar
Or for the saturation of pride
Divine to the mind
Poison for the spirit
People might not want to hear it
But that recognition, they could rewind
And continue to play that all day
Not realizing that an act can be spoiled
While bathing in self-induced glory
Changing a good person in heart
One who used to check positive for morals
Into one who checks negative
The thrill of victory
And the fear of defeat
It is often what drives a competitor to a costly reteat
Be it for love
Sexual or emotional need
Or for strength
Off such things some people do feed
Comprehending such people can be quite an unnatural feat
But this world is driven by pleasures of the flesh
Which is why we all compete

Blind eyes Deaf ears
Tired from a long days work
The man had visited the local bar
He needed a place to ease his sorrows
Just wanted that dreadful day to run into tomorrow
He stumbles into the door
Feels a shove
He shouts what the **** you do that for

His lonely wife was worried
Afraid for his safety
How was she to know he wasn't somewhere buried?

His adrenaline rushed
Attempts to control his drunken anger failed
To dangerous heights their argument sailed
Blind to each other's opinions
Deaf to one another's silent cries

His vision was blurred
Judgment tattered
He would never have thought it
But his wife he had battered
Tears, pride wouldn't allow her to shed
She believed that would give him satisfaction in his head
Truth be told it was something that he dread
Tried to apologize
Had heard of men who beat and cheat many times
He just knew he wasn't one of those guys
This freak accident became a sort of routine
Blind to her bruises
Deaf to her screams

His pride wouldn't let him believe
He would wrongfully harm the mother of his seeds
Alcohol and bottled up emotion
Formula for a love/hate potion
New version of Jeckel and Hyde
This disguise gave his memory a place to hide
How in the world could he deny
His shame, the nights he cried
Caught in a web woven in self pity and hate
Often turned making love, into a revolting form of marital rape
This man is lost to reality as well as to his wife
In his mind, away from him she had no life
She left for the sake of their children
As anger towards his kids was silently building
He called every night and wrote every day
Hoping she would accept him back one day

But it was too late
No more rape
No more screams
No nights crying
Begging for not her sake but the seeds
For them she still had hopes, still had dreams
He was scared and lonely
She was his one and only
She was no longer blind to the problem
No longer deaf to her own conscious to solve them
He was far from sane without her
No longer there to release his stress
No one to help ease his sorrows
Lost sight of his own tomorrow's
Depression takes control
So one night he takes a midnight stroll
Though it was cold he walked in his robe
Found a little pawn shop down on 28th street
Purchased a glock, and one bullet,
With his golden chain as his fee
In this world he felt he could no longer be
When he returned home he saw her standing by the door
His beautiful wife his earlier plan was easily ignored
Blind to his problems
Deaf to the fact they can't be easily ignored

Pity was easily accepted as love
She came back; her only good reason was "just cause"
It was all love; the family had never been so close
Decided to celebrate, too bad they did so with a toast
One glass became two, then, "Are you going to finish that boo"
Four bottles gone, now what can she do
She trusted too soon
And after a month
He was on the same stuff
Instead of his fists, with his glock he would bluff
Frightened for her life, she'd do what he said
One-night things got so bad,
He hit his son for running into his leg
It was apparent to his wife that he had to be put in a body bag
Words were vulgar and enraged
She threw knives she threw blades
Never again
Staying with you has got to be a sin
Her cries were heard
He stopped in his tracks
Cause while she was talking to him
He saw his own reflection in the mirror standing behind her back
Saw what he was, the honest truth, nothing but ugliness inside
Something that drugs and alcohol could never hide
She left with her children, and true to her word stayed gone
And the man took his glock, and eased his pain
But without a better example his son might one-day sing the same song

Nurture
A breast to a baby
Similac for the modern child
Production of milk
A newborns first instinct and know how
To devour nutrients and vitamins, from their provider
It's not just survival, or a means to an end
The start of the beginning determines the road towards the end
This is by definition the role of one or more persons
The love of anyone caring for a daughter
Or a newborn baby son
According to most the job has come to be the woman's
Since her creation
Before the beginning of cities
When there wasn't a definition of civilization
Women alone have become a living revelation
Of things to come
The being has been responsible for nurturing entire nations
From one woman all of this love did come
The love of a mother for the life she birthed
Spanning from before the time of conception
Until the dust is buried in the dirt.

Generational

Conceived by shadows that cling to gene and spirit
Fallen ones gave him hugs
Untrained to the appearance
Unlearned to the experience
He lacked the true nature of love
And so it was
He was drafted
First among sadness
An honor
Plus a pity
Disaster was his day
And shadow filled dreams were his nights
A man on his own
With a hole in his soul
Nothing could ever fill the void
Not the drink not the smoke
But the lust took control
His passion he wore upon his sleeve
He knew not the Father
But, was encouraged by his dad
To not eliminate but spread the sadness
And so he took what he understood as passion
And spread it as far as reach could grasp
Casting his unhappiness upon those
With which he'd become one
But after he got with one He felt the pressure of ten
Not just the weight of the women
But the weight of the lovers they'd been with
He understood not that he was
Violently Violating
The original agenda
Taking on many ideals and thoughts not his own
He had faint visions of happiness
But never tasting of true splendor
All alone
So his hunger grew
Expanding the emptiness
Adding to the wretchedness
That man is born with
Supplementing truth with
Things that left him hopeless

As years progressed
Shadows became thicker
Clarity a thought forgotten
Sleep induced by pills, or drinking
Waking to a pool of tear
Wondering if his life was in vain
What can a man do
Where can a man go
What can a man accomplish
That won't one day fade away, without God?

Second Skin

First appearance means nothing. For looks can deceive, easily leading a person to believe what and only what the other wants them to see. Looking with eyes alone is like the cord missing from a telephone, obsolete and incomplete in every way. It takes more to see what's beneath the surface. What's seemingly quite a find can turn out to be a three-ring circus. Mostly everything can be seen through who a person is how they talk, their conversation, how they live. Lies often contradict, and those who use alcohol to often get lit, have issues that must be dealt with before entering any type of relationship. It's impossible to perceive that a person's problem will eventually leave on its own. Take my word it gets hard to stay with someone who isn't on the same tone, of advancement and enlightenment. Because if a person isn't doing any thing to improve his/her situation, his/her mind, time is something they are wasting. What a person really is will always be found inside. Once you learn how to find what's behind a cute smile the better off you will be. I pray you don't get caught up in lust, a powerful sight and touch spirit/emotion. It leads to devotion to those deceptive surfaces, be aware and look lively for everything has a purpose.

Ken's Prayer

My name is ken and Lord I'm a sinner
I am a wretch
Not deserving the crumbs from your dinner
I'm hoping
I'm praying O' Lord for another chance
I think I used up all my credits
But Of your mercy I'd like a grant
I've had too many days like today
My friend just got shot
Three days before his birthday
Two days before mine
By today I figured this world would have been mine
We sold a little something, and only you know the rest
I feel so trapped, trying to constantly re-up
This is hopeless
It's been years, measured in tears
Wells been dry, so now I measure in tattoos
Can't retain focus
I know now I need you
I found a Bible
And now I see that I am through
Because I've been reading your book all day
You are far from like the rest,
Most people are just surface
You told me I'm worth something
That even I have a purpose
And on top of all that I have Dominion
Now I see
I spoke into my life the hardships that I have been living
From my first sale on the block
Until my friend was found lying on the red stained ground
My name is in your hand, you said no one else deserved it
I cursed your name
And begged forgiveness
You threw it into the sea of forgetfulness
My life is yours the choice is mine
My choice is you
My choice is real
Now I can live

Buried Alive
When Sam was a boy he was happy just playing with his toys
Like most kids he was shy, fiend for sweets and hardly ever lied
Kind in Heart fragile in mind,
A child's mind is clay
Impressionable,
The canvas of life
As he grew older things became complicated
He didn't know how to approach new people,
And old friendships became outdated,
In his life video games became overrated
They consumed his mind, left his body in aftershock,
His mama couldn't get him outside, not even for a stroll around the block
No fresh air
In the same condition were his only friends
It seemed a sort of torture that only he could end
Closed himself off from others,
It hurt
Can't you see the pain in his eyes?
He didn't know it but he was buried alive
So if you see him extend your arm and shake his hand
Let him: know he's not alone in his struggle,
Survival depends upon a helping hand.
Please don't let him die by his own hand for the lack of a friend.

Real
If thought were to become reality
Real
That would be a fantasy
Love and no hurt
Real
Would leave no one longing for that 6 feet
A desire to return to the earth
Pleasure without pain
Real
You can run all you want to
But even a thin man can't avoid the rain
Action without thought
A conscious is how you feel
But sometimes it has to be bought
Real
That is where that pain comes in to play
And separates that imagination
From that other place
It is known by most
That place they call
Real

This world

How can we sustain a world of hate, a world of pain
Ground littered, and saturated with acid rain
Where all good gestures seem in vain
Do we have the right to complain,
Damage is advancing beyond the rate of change
Earthquakes shake beneath us; the earth involuntarily provides us,
With the power and minerals we need to succeed,
In the art of divide and conquer
The earth cries out during storms,
It's tired of being our wars' sponsors
This world, is overcome with the dirt that we do
This world, it takes a toll on mortal man, and all that exist too
This world, the heavens above rain down on our behalf
This world, on the trails of ghost slave ships hurricanes dash
Problems we still have today, existed in the past
How long can we last
There is no victory until our last breath
Only peace to be found seems accompanied by death
We are forced to find meaning in life
While most around simply exist and act trife
So cling to your good memories,
For when the world turns on you,
It will be your remedy
Your very soul will constantly be twisted and twirled
Have faith; because only God can save you from this world

Time

Something forgotten
When against, it's pretty much a lost cause
Battling something that's irreversible, not interchangeable
It can't be stolen, changed, or booked
The very thought of such things should pierce your mind and body
Freezing your soul leaving you shook
Right or wrong right or wrong that same old song right or wrong
But that song is incomplete
Yeah, it might have a beautiful chorus
With a timber beat
It's the formula to a good song
The same goes for this planet we spend a very short time on
You can add or subtract it right or wrong right or wrong
Plain and simply it's a busted equation, lacking information
Please come to the realization
That time is something a person can't depend on
Nor do we posses the power to prolong
Of time you will always be a victim
But age only takes a toll on our worldly systems
Time is better spent to overcome defeat for the thrill of victory
Wanting, wishing, praying to one day live on past centuries
The key is the Bible I am a witness
Gods' word put content in me
Just believe in the savior Jesus Christ
He will open your eyes and allow you to see
Extinguishing the darkness with light
Age and a short life can make you a victim of time
But eternal bliss is waiting for you
All it takes is devotion to God, seed faith, and just a little of your time

Irony

Time for you to back away
This isn't for show; it's here to spray
Mostly plastic so it couldn't be detected
I'm simply hear to see my cause is respected
If it wasn't for men like you
The skies in my hood would still be blue
We wouldn't have to hide from rain mixed with acid.
And when I walk the streets I wouldn't be stepping on any trash kid
Time for your existence to be blasted away
No more strikes, no more conferences could make all this mess okay
Your heart is beating too fast I can feel it
Regardless, your wig I'm about to peel it
Suddenly I see pain in your eyes
You grab your chest
Before I knew it you'd fallen out into cardiac arrest
The stress was too much for your heart to take
Why just now realize that you've made mistakes
Tried to bounce but the jakes was on me
Knew for sure I would suffer the fate of any jury
Made up my mind in a rush, I had no choice but to hurry
Decided by my own hands, not theirs would I be buried.
Said a quick prayer squeeze the trigger, then I died
Only to wake up in a lake fire starring into the man I killed eyes'

Therapy
Feet firm against fragments of broken glass and memory
Hands designed for greatness, placed
Palms first against a wall of brick
Cold to the touch
Something faint
With a scent
With a face that can't be seen
And the tears roll along cheeks
Leaping sacrificially toward the ground
Littered by broken glass
Those drops of salt based relief
Begin to mix with the glass
Changing its molecular structure into that of flesh and blood
A creature is formed, with the likeness of a venomous snake
Cocked and bent on striking
It smiles at first
Then it laughs
With venom dripping around feet
From each drop a child springs up
Giving voice to a chant
Saying: "ask *not, tell not*"
A question is echoing in the distance
But the children get louder
Ask not tell not
5
The questions stop
4
The children disappear
3
The snake turns back into tears
2
The wall begins to shake
1
The shrink says wake and feel refreshed

God is love

God is love
All love under him must begin with him
I did not know this
My perception of love was pleasure
Physical
Emotional
I was unaware that it was all spiritual
I believed that as long as I cared for a woman
That it was okay to lay with her
And that I wouldn't lay with anyone
Unless I felt like I could have a child with her
I had it all twisted
Because the wages of sin are death
That's why people have S.T.D.'s from fornication
That's why smokers get lung cancer
And so on And so on
I thank God that I stopped when I did
Lust was consuming me,
Clouding my vision
Searing my conscious, as to avoid guilt
Until through the boards of my burdens,
The light of God seeped through
In this chapter, progression is most evident
My thought process did a complete turn around
Now written
For all to see

Turning Points of Love

Can u feel it
The music streamlines your body
A gentle breeze in its entirety
Can u feel it
It's difficult I know
To let it all go and let loose
Relaxing and *freely flowing*
Like a hot day and a cold juice
Can u feel it
The very tingles in your spine
That touch you're feeling is mine
Please don't hide behind silence
I'm assured that u will break it to my compliance
I have a want; no I've got a need
To cause a quivering in those knees
Not stopping until I succeed
Can u feel it
This night is coming to a close
But let's not close it
Let's open it and welcome the night
Underneath the deep dark sky
While being christened in the moons light
To tell the truth these things won't take place every night
But that vibe, that vibe is everlasting
Surpassing limits and boundaries
If you're ever in need, you know where to find me
Close your eyes and you will be filled with the entire essence of me
Can u feel it

Captivating

I could be admiring a statue
I could be looking at the most beautiful hue of blue
True enough, I could be witness to a falling star
Watching rainbows embracing cloud tops after the rains came
Or seeing horses running free, before they were tamed
A star being born could catch my eye through a telescope
While catching the joy of lovers that simply had to elope
I could see the moon fade, and the very planets rearrange
But to you if it's all the same
I know where my interest lies
And I could just as well, be more than satisfied starring into your eyes

Personal Ads
SBM Seeking SBF

Walk with dignity
Knowledge in speech
Healthy in body
Worthy in spirit
Silly at times
Not too deep
At times a little nasty
No raunch if you please
One hand on my chest
The other in my hair
Sex isn't necessary
Just to be fair
I'm the 'whatever type'
Be who you are
For real!
And love will go far
Appreciate my talents
But give the glory to God
Work to show improvement
Meaning handle you business
Of African decent
Single
And ready for love
Not to get too picky
And above all believe in something greater
Than love
Than the earth
Than the stars
Then under God all we need will be ours

Crazy that way
Fingertips used for gentleness
Entire hand used to caress
Imagination, for time and space to disappear
Creating the illusion, No the reality that no one else is near
Fear has no place, even though you've lost your way
For you are lost on purpose
Love's just crazy that way
Clouds take shape
Beautiful objects catch your eye
For no reason at all you purchase things you would never buy
Candles used for lighting and scent
Champagne is no longer an excuse to get bent
Rather to set the mood
For love
Gentle
        Forbidden
Patient
        Blinding
Desired
Consuming
And so complete
It's as pure and as forgotten as a sunray,
Descending from the heavens
Love's just crazy that way

Tonight

It is on nights like tonight
That men of fortune
Would surrender all they own
To find jewel as precious as you
It's on nights like tonight
That purpose unfolds
And as concrete turns cold
It sparks off streetlights
Making broken glass shine like glitter
Near the gutters
A sea of beauty
No names, no introduction
Only salutations, and conversation
On nights like tonight
I await your next word

My only Seed
I found a seed one day
And off love it grew
Whatever that seed desired
No doubt I would do
Gave it food from my plate
Water from my cup
This seed was quite a find
Chances of finding it was more than luck
I was stuck in a web of patience and desire
Got to keep it close don't want this seed to expire
With time it grew, nothing without this seed would I want to do
Connected by the tails of our eternal souls
Fast and bold did this seed grow
Entangled its roots in the very base of my heart
Got me wondering without this root how did the beat of it start
Unlike any before I held it above
Can't believe, but in such a short time it grew into this feeling called love

Stimulating

I looked into her eyes and saw where truth lies
She had me trapped with her beauty, this doesn't happen usually
She has me fenced
And I can't figure out what in the world it could be
Body smelled of peaches, lips tasted of sweetness
If there was a revival,
She'd be the preacher and I'd be her witness
When our hands touch it creates the feeling of fresh linen,
If they had sheets like that, you could always tell what bed I'm in
When she opens her mouth, out comes the sweetest sound
Light accent, articulate with the sound of the south,
Now isn't that profound
She touched the core of me; she wasn't just a score to me
If I was forced to measure her on a scale of 1 to 10,
A hundred is what the score would be
Maybe infinity
For we are destined for all of earth's time
I'm satisfied, because whenever we date
It's not sexual, yet and still
Each and every pore on my body is what she stimulates

Mind Erection
Freedom from the physical
Concentrating on embracing the mental
Now that's sensual
My ideal mind erection
A woman who of her mind uses every section
With a thought process that will give, and have direction
Leaving no room for common reality
Only the one that we create would matter to me
Just as one has to open their mouth to taste
The same is done with the expression of thought
Doing so would win battles without them having to be fought
My ideal mind erection
Goes beyond the need for feelings protection
Beyond love- physical and mental
A highway from heaven
Spiritual
Beyond trust- surpassing the need to sexually burst
Beyond the comfort, and sadness of hiding myself
Far beyond money
For I know my happiness won't be found in wealth
Rather my true sunlight,
Will be as beautiful as the sun setting
1 woman will posses it
She will be my ideal mind erection

Promise symbol
In your presence
I am reminded of covenants
God's promise
For truth is in his word
I asked and I received you
With all your Fire
With all your love
As precious as the promise symbol
Changing my countenance
To that which accompanies a pair of dimples
My desire is your hand
And my demand is in myself
Making sure off of nine you will rarely land
The reflection of your worth by me
Would appear as the spectrum
Many colors in thee
Man makes things complicated
Reality is meant to be more simple
You are a gift from above
As beautiful, and as precious as the promise symbol

Majesty

You massage my universe
Leaving the world at peace
In your footprints
I can see the difference
Between little girls and majesty
Your mystery is what defines me
And my devotion is what binds me
My imagination leads…
Being that I can see God in you
And I can feel God in me
Love being a bridge
There aren't just two in love there's three
I liken you unto food on my table
I liken you unto water from my cup
In order for me to continue to be happy
Daily from you my soul must sup
That's why I see all things being possible
Like for the sun to shine in the midst of the rain
Mountains reflecting off rivers that put mirrors to shame
Or the possibility
That one soul could occupy the bodies of two
Only to come together making one again
That's where you and I come in
And where is it that you and I end
Between you and I there is no end
Between you and I
Between you and I is something
That gives sight to the blind
Saturates deserts, and leaves dew drops on fields
It can tear down barriers, and build
Building futures
What we have is faith, what we have is love
What you have is me
What I have is a woman
Woman meaning from man
Before you birthed me I birthed you
You are my equal
The future mother of my kids
My hearts protection, you are
You are my rib

Made Complete - (lighting of the candles)
Take some time to feel this moment in its entirety
Clear your mind,
And witness love ascend from the skies
As flames are ignited
Candles begin burn
And wax gently begins to liquefy
What were once 2 is now becoming 1
Instead of subtraction
It is the creation of something new
Not limited by worldly actions
Made complete under God,
Now that is true passion
Not upon a mountain of sand
But at the top of a rock
Creating a balance
Still, this is not where their reach stops
For their souls rooted in the Father
Temples standing strong
While His word branches out
Providing other people with plenty of shade
It should never be a question why marriage is heavenly ordained
For God's plans are beyond our understanding
Prayer will be their counselor
So that blessings have a place to be landing
Those flames belong to them
Lighting their way through darkness
All of these things you might not be able to envision
Engulfed in this blessed union
Your heart must be open in order for you to see
The melting and creation of a new light
The very beginning of a new journey for Tonja and Lee

Just thinking
If I had to I'd wait for you
If I had to I'd watch as every grain
Slipped through the hour glass of life
Being patient as does Christ just for your hand
If I had my choice I'd wait by a river as a plant
Loc's spread beyond the length of my cuticle
Representing my roots
Reaching for you
My affections nourishment
I try to control my thoughts
But each thought of you is like
Each thought of you is like
My every thought of you gets stuck on repeat
It's almost like
I can see pleasure and taste defeat
As I breathe in wind and whisper your name
And I must repent for this pedestal on which I place you
These treasures buried inside hinder my steps
They can only be smiles with teeth clenched to prevent
Unloosed words from falling like rain
Rather than water
Liquid silk that accompanies a moment
Like when we stare with no words
Silent became the rivers
Silent became the trees
Fluttering like little hummingbirds
Where our hearts
And far from narrow was the path upon which our thoughts traveled
So I, So I
So I had to take what we thought was the truth
And substitute it with the only thing I knew was true
We charmed each other
Beyond the point of easy retrieval
In my mind I could paint you without a brush
Pen paper or easel
Sure we could have easily tried to jack and Jill our way up the hill
To fetch a pail of spirit, only to make our way back uneasily down that hill
Knowing that it was not our time nor was it Gods will
But if I had to I'd wait for you,
If I had to I'd watch as every grain
Slipped through the hour glass of life
Being patient as does Christ just for your hand
If I had to
I'd just be
I'd just be thinking of you

I can see
Apart you and I have known without knowing
Together perhaps, we shall see without seeing
A fabric sown together with patches that stretch
Beyond this second, beyond this minute,
Beyond this hour, beyond our time
If time would allow
And you would permit me
I would throw caution to the wind
And unleash this gift I have been given to love you
I have met three or four along the way
If you would forgive me
For in them I only saw pieces of you
But coming face to face with the entire puzzle
Humbles me
We have hardly even begun
And you have peeled back layers of reinforced steel
Treated wood, and roadblocks
With barrels filled with water, orange cones, and signs that read
Dead end, yield, stop, and don't touch me, don't touch me, don't touch me
To reveal a heart that pumps blood to the rhythm of your walk
To show a smile so broad that dimples form whenever you talk
Or stare, or come close,
Enough to press your shoulder next to mine
Taking it slow as to not expose your treasure prematurely
I anticipate
The arrival of heavens decision
And embrace patience
Rather than your lonely nights
I taste of contentment
Rather than of your lips
My concern is about the state of your soul
As opposed to just getting in-between those hips
No, because…
I could see you before we ever did meet
I can feel you, your soul signature are inherently unique
I must have been blind before you
Because I can see now this very second why I was supposed to wait
There is never a minute I spend with you and I feel like it went to waste
It feels like a shower every hour I spend with you
Pure and Godly intentions, holy commune is all that we do
I don't feel lost anymore, and neither do you
Not out of place anymore
This time around I feel like I have a clue
This life is short
And I can see clearly
The path is rough
But it would be smoother if only you'd walk with me

About the Author

Joe Gofoe II was born and raised in Grand Rapids MI. A student and fan of poetry Joe has been writting poetry for 10 years. Though he has only been performing for 4 years, he speaks with a passion unquenchable. His desire is to please God with his words, as well as how he lives his life. So that it will not be him, but the God in him that will be remembered

Notes

Notes

Notes

Printed in the United States
127600LV00004B/4/P

9 781434 377845